We Are Just Human

The Poetry Book

Because We Are Edition

By

Raven Lotus Crow

<u>Forward</u>

I've finally fixed all of the glaring problems this book had when it was first released. No longer will I trust another to proofread what I can do on my own.

This is the way it was supposed to be when it was first made with a little changes to the sentence structures and corrected spelling of words.

Please enjoy the Because We Are Edition, the true edition that composites my vision and brings it to life.

Raven

Dedicated to my friends and the program I attend.
Without you I would be lost. For that I am very grateful
for you.

If you find yourself in need of help.

Just seek it and you shall find it!

Christopher Scott Whittle

A.K.A.

Raven Lotus Crow

<u>Content</u>

By
Raven Lotus Crow

Like looking out at the open sea
Just my calm and me
Like the beauty of a sunrise
Like my feelings for guys
Content I am with life
Content I am forevermore
Content I am with Life
Now time to open up the door

<u>The Wind</u>

By
Raven Lotus Crow

Ever changing with a whim
With changing dialed to the brim
With all new things big and small
As you would know if you were tall
The storm rages on and brings the wind
As life goes on and is kind
As many ways are open and bind
The wind is friend
Yet can be foe
Which one will be at your door

<u>Everybody Matters</u>

By
Raven Lotus Crow

When someone is in trouble
Do they make it double
Do they take the time
To change at the cost of a dime
To think that you are the only one special
Leads to misguided faith and the Devil
Are you sure not everybody matters
For I disagree as your point staggers
Look around we are one
Look around and see we are done
Put away the hate
Before It is too late

<u>Kerosine</u>

By
Raven Lotus Crow

As sadness and despair take you
You feel stuck like glue
How does it feel taking blame
Hot as a flame
Like pouring kerosine on a fire
Everything is more than dire
Your love and passion feel dead
As if buried in lead
A shot to the heart
No more new passion and start
All you can think is, why me
Then the answer comes, just let it be

<u>Passion</u>

By

Raven Lotus Crow

As bright as the sun

With as much fun

Where life begins and prevails

When there are no fails

When planets align

Where the sea meets the shoreline

When you can be yourself

At last, put the bad feelings on the shelf

There is no place for the inner fire of despair

No more of it not even enough to harm another hair

<u>We Are Not So Different</u>

By
Raven Lotus Crow

God sees his followers and smiles
As for many just like me the Goddess lives in our
lifestyles
We all live on this Earth to give good will
No need to give a bill
Nature is what God made
And nature is where the Goddess stayed
We are all human and made of flaws
No one is chasing everyone with claws
If we can find common ground
We will be forever around

<u>The Fey</u>

By
Raven Lotus Crow

Little trickster yet beautiful and strange
How you never seem to change
You show us magick
Without a stick
Will you show us life
Or threaten us with a knife
Will we go on a trip to Neverland
Or plunge from the skies as planned
Little trickster with a fiddle
You can not keep anyone imprisoned in the middle

<u>The One</u>

By
Raven Lotus Crow

Boy, you are like summer rain
Boy, you are not vain
Everytime I look into your eyes
You are more important than other guys
Your breath is like the sea
A wind blowing you to me
If there was a way to say I am done
I would say you are the one

<u>Phoenix</u>

By

Raven Lotus Crow

From fiery death and dance
Such a beautiful romance
We all are born from the ashes
And life ends as if with matches
Like a mighty bird
Just say the word
We burn quite brighter
Like a flame from a lighter

<u>The Force</u>

By
Raven Lotus Crow

When all is lost there is light
All it asks for is not might
When you need peace to be
Think of all and not just of me
Too much of one can be bad
To go the dark side just use mad
To go light don't use might
Letting go brings you to the light

<u>Life</u>

By
Raven Lotus Crow

It breathes a breath of renewal
As if you were in a school
Love and bliss in the air
Like the wind in your hair
Dancing clumsy throughout the day
Like the beautiful month of May
As you see what it brings
Counting the tree rings

<u>Death</u>

By
Raven Lotus Crow

It creeps up eventually
Nothing can prepare you mentally
Loss is not the end
Time to let things mend
All the sorrow in the world
Can't bring them back that is the word
Instead embrace their love
Send them off like a dove

<u>Grandiosity</u>

By
Raven Lotus Crow

Who am I today
A wizard I must say
Talking nonsense all the time
Like trying to pay bills with just a dime
A darker feeling grows stronger
Somethings wrong, why bother
A shadow creeps and slithers in
It's a demon and it says, let me in

<u>The Break Down</u>

By
Raven Lotus Crow

I am not fine
How could you be so out of line
I have seen you yet again
Why do you seek to hurt me, I refrain
Like a piece of broken glass
You are not aloud near me not in class
Ex-boyfriend you do me harm
You are not my friend and not warm

<u>Nightmare</u>

By
Raven Lotus Crow

Like the times when advice falls short
Like trying to help a friend and the abort
When all things go to hell
What else can I tell
Everytime I go out of my way
I get slapped and mentally I stay
I try to give you love
But all you do is bit the head off the dove

<u>A Friend</u>

By
Raven Lotus Crow

Who is the person with good advice
Someone who is not a vice
Someone who cares and warm
Someone who does not bring harm
All the people who say they care
You know they will always be there
As with the rise of the sun
They will be there and never done

<u>Mary J.</u>

By
Raven Lotus Crow

As if a weight is lift off of me
I just want to let it be
I feel absolutely relaxed
All my feelings are laxed
I do not feel pain
I do not refrain
It is here I must say
It is here and here to stay

<u>Pride</u>

By
Raven Lotus Crow

I have love for who I am
Why do other just want to slam
The world has gone mad
Seeing those of my community put to death is sad
Why not show pride
Not every guy has a bride
As the world heals
There will be many deals

<u>My Team</u>

By
Raven Lotus Crow

Pride and joy at seeing them win
No more losing, for what a sin
I see them do so well
All I want is to ring the church bell
For the trophy is getting nearer
Like seeing something much clearer
Like seeing the marvels
Here it is to The Devils

<u>Sparrow</u>

By
Raven Lotus Crow

My little friend how you fly
To see you so high
Outstretched wings spread so far
Love to see you even more
Flying so gracefully
It's you against the sea
Above the land you can be
With the sir and with me

<u>Fox</u>

By
Raven Lotus Crow

Cleaver beautiful friend
You are here and you are then
You of red and white and black
I know you have my back
With your cunning insight
Knowledge is more than might
Living where you must
Being sought is such a bust

<u>Gems</u>

By
Raven Lotus Crow

You look of such beauty
You are found amongst pirate booty
With colors shining bright
Even better in the light
So beautiful when worn
Is very beautiful as shone
I adore you more
So be it forevermore

<u>The Sea</u>

By
Raven Lotus Crow

You are such a mystery
You seem to be
All is ups and downs
Be careful or you will drown
Have you been strong or weak
Have you been nothing but meak
Your deeps know no bounds
Even deeper than the ground

<u>Betrayal</u>

By
Raven Lotus Crow

You said you are doing bad
I try to help you when you are sad
I give you my heart
Yet you stab it with a dart
How can I trust you
How far can I, the length of a shoe
I feel the weight on my back
It’s like you said, you like that

<u>Hope</u>

By
Raven Lotus Crow

When all else fails
Good will trails
When darkness grows
But then light shows
When you lose faith and love seems dim
Life shows up and is of a brim
When all feels like chains and locks
Remember it was last in Pandora's Box

<u>I Am Just Human</u>

By
Raven Lotus Crow

We all make mistakes
It's just the wrong actions, it takes
We all love
When we do it soars like a dove
We all feel hate
Let it not become your fate
Emotions do run wild
Run as fast as a child

<u>Anger</u>

By
Raven Lotus Crow

When you are wronged and are blamed
How your emotions run wild like an out-of-control
flame
How when you help someone and they spit it back in
your face
How you feel like a total disgrace
When all anyone does is just yell
It all feel like you are burning in Hell
You just hold it in until you cant
Fiery breath will make them feel like an ant

Being A Nerd

By
Raven Lotus Crow

Comic Books and Superheroes
Are fun, not zeros
DND night and we are around the table
Do not worry Mage, the horses are in the stable
Having fun with friends
This never has any ends
Mess with one and get all
Doesn't matter if you are small or tall

<u>Dragon</u>

By
Raven Lotus Crow

Pretty fiery beast
How the knight is but a feast
Blamed for the princess and her village
Why not blame it on the pillage
With a beautiful massive body and wings
Sitting on top of treasure and rings
The treasure you guard it
But failed when against a hobbit

<u>Homeless</u>

By
Raven Lotus Crow

When all goes to Hell
There is not much to tell
Surviving is but a necessary thing
All hope feels lost and doesn't mean a thing
But I tell you keep looking up
This hopelessness needs to stop
When your success began
I am already your greatest fan

<u>Mutt</u>

By
Raven Lotus Crow

I am a mix
And don't need to be fixed
I come from many walks of life
Boy, it feels like strife
With all that come together to make me
I will only plea
Be happy who you are as a one
It is all we are and done

<u>Koi</u>

By

Raven Lotus Crow

Dancing in the waves below
The balance of life is slow
Yin and Yang is in the balance
As if watching heaven's palace
Tails and bodies so gracefully
In a dance indefinitely
Living in a mysterious dance
See them at a glance

<u>Happy I Stay</u>

By
Raven Lotus Crow

Warm puppies on your lap
Ice tea and a map
A map with your trip planned out
You and your significant other with a shout
They stay by your side
Love is in the air
The sea is yours and you are there

<u>Ships</u>

By
Raven Lotus Crow

Beautiful shaped pieces of wood
With everything constructed so good
Built on the land then sent out to the sea
It's a new journey
Captain signals his crew
They listen as the whistle blew
Off to the sea and to the next port
Off to see the next fort

<u>My Guitar</u>

By
Raven Lotus Crow

Ode to my love and passion
Oh you are my main attraction
Making fantastic sounds
Oh there will be no bounds
Loving music ever more
Using any opportunity like an open door
Making music for those to adore
Only this I wish and nothing more

<u>Video Games</u>

By
Raven Lotus Crow

It's yet another level
Time to hit the dirt and the gravel
Swing swords and rescuing the princess
Looks like she's in another castle, with distress
Be yourself or and character built
There will be no such guilt
Lose all of your lives
Time to beat this game with many survives

<u>Trek</u>

By
Raven Lotus Crow

Ode to the pioneer of SciFi
Where would we be without that guy
Going bravely to the stars
Going farther pass even Mars
Look at what was made
Couldn't be more saved
From legendary show
Shame it became more of a blow

<u>Hero</u>

By
Raven Lotus Crow

For those who fight for us
For those who seek justice
For those who heal the sick
For those who are last pick
I give a shout to the brave
Who save us all from an early grave
For those great and small
We could not have done it without you all

<u>Filk</u>

By
Raven Lotus Crow

Tell me the tale of the man
Who saw the princess from his plan
He fought the dragon and got her
To bad he found another
The guitar play and we jam
The song come together at The Clam
All our nerdy fans come one and all
To hear the tale of Sir. Paul

<u>Al</u>

By
Raven Lotus Crow

Whenever I am down and need a laugh
You always pull through on my behalf
With genius ways with words
Being one with us nerds
Play a polka and I adore
Play another we want more
You are the best to make us laugh
Thanks again for your autograph

<u>Freddie</u>

By
Raven Lotus Crow

You had a beautiful voice
You were a man with rejoice
When you sang we crowded
As we sang with you we became unclouded
Bringing us more anthems and making us belong
Stomping our feet to the drum
You left us to early on
We will remember you forever on

Medicine

By

Raven Lotus Crow

What keeps me stable
For giving me a chance to be able
Take the pills with a drink
After that see the shrink
So I am being really safe
So it shall be my failsafe
Seeing everything as it stands
Keep to the pills and the plans

<u>Water</u>

By
Raven Lotus Crow

Bland as hell without any taste
We still need you even on our face
I drink you with Mio
Drinking you and listening to Dio
You cover this world
Home to most of the microworld
Clear as the morning dew
Drink more you know you need to

<u>Lucas</u>

By
Raven Lotus Crow

You brought us something that is divine
All six movies I can define
Staring from the end and ending in the beginning
Remember teddy bears singing
With so much diversity
As much or even more than a University
You brought us even more
Every film of your I adore

<u>The Rainbow</u>

By
Raven Lotus Crow

Little children and adults love you alike
Seeing you in the sky as we bike
Such a problem with some fools
Did they get an F in their schools
Why show such beauty hate
Did they seriously think of it, mate
It is not only for the gays
Hate is stupid and never pays

Owl

By
Raven Lotus Crow

Being nocturnal and cleaver
No one can see you easily ever
Turning you head around
Like The Exorcist cursing abound
Voice like a demonic ghost
We look for it past the post
Wisdom of the ages
Familiars to Mages

Take A Drive

By
Raven Lotus Crow

Life is too fast
So make it last
When you feel stuck
Get yourself out of a rut
It sounds easy but it is not
To find yourself again with a new start
Take the keys and get in
Be careful as the wheels spin

<u>Unfair</u>

By
Raven Lotus Crow

Knowing a friend that has died
Having spoke to someone and have lied
All the deeds that came untrue
All of them seems to be you
Letting all of life pass by
Not being able to say goodbye
Knowinging all that you know is wrong
Being unable to protect those from a gun

<u>Manic Day</u>

By
Raven Lotus Crow

When I feel most high
As if I could reach the sky
Life is but a joke
Taking it too easy as I spoke
Seeing things with a new start
Sometimes it will come apart
When grandiosity rears its ugly head
Time to strap me to a bed

<u>TMZ</u>

By
Raven Lotus Crow

Why do we need to see
More bothered celebrity
Why do you want to intrude
Don't you think you are rude
Go back to school and find a new job
Before you create an angry mob
All your program is sad
All you do is make us mad

<u>Old Norse</u>

By
Raven Lotus Crow

A language that is soothing yet harsh
Something you can picture with a creepy marsh
The people so fierce
With a sword they will pierce
Look out for the North men
They come to pillage again
With ships so lean and long
They brought us sights and sense of belong

<u>Auld English</u>

By
Raven Lotus Crow

A language so different from present
Like comparing penguins to pheasants
Some so auld
That it has its own mold
Being the beginning transformation to now
And sounding nothing close, but how
Its origins are germanic in nature
I gave one in this feature

Sakura (Cherry Blossom)

By
Raven Lotus Crow

Beautiful flowers in bloom
How many of shades of pink have room
Gorgeous sight to behold
They flower in DC I have been told
Native tree to Japan
Makes the most beautiful and gran
That tune about it by far
Is the most recognizable so far

<u>Professor Jones</u>

By
Raven Lotus Crow

With a fedora and a whip
You make Nazis cry and go limp
Beating them up and protecting the world
You are more a man and that’s my word
Stopping fools from using the Box
Chasing Nazis and outsmarting them like a fox
Going on adventure with your dad
Ending up in Mayan ruins instead

<u>Tropical Forest</u>

By
Raven Lotus Crow

Something that should be preserved
Something that other deserve
Somewhere where mystery lies
Somewhere where the land cries
All we do is burn it down
We are nothing but about to drown
Let's save it before it's to late
Let's not give up on its fate

Lithium

By
Raven Lotus Crow

When I felt down I went low
When I started not to be able to tow
When I died I lived
What else can I give
Sweet serenity I would want
For all of my pain would be blunt
Living like the dead
Can give you such dread

<u>Lying Is Such A Waste</u>

By
Raven Lotus Crow

Why do people lie
To protect the next guy
Or is it for selfish gain
Or to give as much pain
Whatever the reason
Stop it now before the next season
For I have done it a lot
It has served me not

<u>Showing Some Class</u>

By
Raven Lotus Crow

Now it's time to be a part of the mass
Time to show some level of class
When the elderly need help
Stop what you are doing to be of help
When you see a wrong being done
Call the police and let them know where you are from
When you get out of your car
Let your other one out even more

<u>Hate Belongs In The Trash</u>

By
Raven Lotus Crow

What is the point of hate
Doesn't it seem to others to just inflate
All of these fools
Stand around and bark orders from stools
Hate brings more pain
Just like an out-of-control train
Time to set the world free
A place safer for you and me

<u>Misheard Lyrics</u>

By
Raven Lotus Crow

Funny meanings behind the words
Makes me laugh uncontrollably because of what I
heard
Goofy misleading facts
Meanings of songs so jacked
Sometimes you are like what the fuck
Now Fear of the Dark is Fear of the DUCK
As to who you can call
It’s those bastards down the hall

<u>Life On Other Worlds</u>

By
Raven Lotus Crow

Can it exist other than here
Yes I believe it is crystal clear
For if there wasn't why the hell not
For wouldn't we be nothing but rot
We who claim the universe as a whole
Doesn't that sound like bull
If we are alone and nothing more
The universe definitely mess this score

<u>Tea</u>

By

Raven Lotus Crow

A drink made for me
Replacing the coffee when it's not free
I don't feel right without a cup
I just need to feel my up
To some it tastes like grass
To others they come in mass
Many flavors to choose from now
Sometimes you need milk from a cow

<u>Anime</u>

By
Raven Lotus Crow

Crazy action and funny lines
Was that character actually blind
Who could eat more Goku or a person who is a cat
Look out for that bat
Animation from Japan
Is more to it to understand
Begin your journey with the basics
All will come alive with the music

<u>Man's Best Friend</u>

By
Raven Lotus Crow

If you want true love
A dog will show you it and above
Dogs are kind
Just keep that in your mind
Not all breeds are bad
You don't know what can make some mad
Pitbulls are the best
Just treat them right like the rest

<u>Squirrel</u>

By
Raven Lotus Crow

Fuzzy wuzzy little ball
How you are cute and small
Love watching you run about
Not a care or a doubt
Being chased by dogs
Running about on some logs
Little tiny ball of fur
How you make us laugh as it were

<u>Having Fun</u>

By
Raven Lotus Crow

Looking out at the sea
Sitting down and being me
Going out to dine
There will be no need for wine
Going to the amusement park
Having a blast right from the start
Life is a bliss
Time's too short to miss

<u>Cryptid</u>

By
Raven Lotus Crow

Did you see something in the lake
Is it real or is it fake
Do serpents live in the sea
Are they bigger than me
Is there something in the dark
Something strolling through the park
Is there something that grows
To this I say, who really knows

<u>Alien</u>

By
Raven Lotus Crow

Are there such things as UFOs
For many would answer, who really knows
I believe we are not alone
For those skeptics I do groan
For if we are alone as I said
What's the point I feel a shed
Of all the nonsense going around
Makes those higher look like a clown

Mark (Sorry For Rian)

By
Raven Lotus Crow

You brought us so much fun
Hope they reboot the trilogy before you are done
Rian made you cry
Rian is not a nice guy
They really made a mistake
When they tried to raise the stake
Episode seven was bad
Because it made you really sad

Hamill

By
Raven Lotus Crow

Brilliant actor has won
Is and forever shall be number one
From Luke to The Joker
Your skills are not mediocre
Hired to voice Skeletor
We the fans call for more
To the greatest guy around
Your care knows no bound

<u>Fear</u>

By
Raven Lotus Crow

When you hear something that's not there
When you feel the standing of your hair
Where ghost get you the most
Isn't wonderful being the host
When all you can do is run
Is everything really that fun
When there is nothing you can do
Where in the darkness, do you feel it too

<u>Pan</u>

By
Raven Lotus Crow

Is he a goat or a man
A horny God of the land
As he is a satyr
Watch out or he will be your mater
As the animals multiply
As their numbers reaches the sky
He smiles and we will fly
He's our special guy

<u>The Bee</u>

By
Raven Lotus Crow

Why don't you see
You just need to let me be
Flying winged danger
I am not a stranger
All of your stings
Bring me next to death and the lesson rings
How can I shout any louder
For I will not be chowder

<u>Wasp</u>

By
Raven Lotus Crow

Evil incarnation with wings
Demonic hellspawn as it sings
What I would do to see you fry
All I want from you is to die
Evil winged demon spawn
How I fear you across the lawn
You can still be bad
You can try to kill me and make me mad

<u>Stuff I Dread</u>

By
Raven Lotus Crow

Like they said about the channel
They said we will cancel
All these kids try to rewrite history
What is with them, it's a mystery
When I support someone who will be canceled
They act like a possessed thing being channeled
Cancel culture please go away
Never come back another day

An Angel In The Sky

By
Raven Lotus Crow

We send you off with as much grace
You will no longer return to this place
You were my family
Mother what happened was a tragedy
Mother you had flaws
But all is in the past and was
I will not forget your smile
You forgave with style
So far what I can say
I only wish you could stay
Broken hearted I am
Crying forevermore where I stand

<u>Freedom</u>

By
Raven Lotus Crow

Feeling of absolute relief
Being free to practice your belief
Having respect for those before
Having that feeling that you are loved more
Seeing all the people just be
Knowing I can be just me
Not many places in the world
Give a darn about the word

<u>Moth</u>

By

Raven Lotus Crow

Little tiny thing
Can be bigger than a ring
Eating the cloth
You are just a moth
As it burns brighter
You are drawn to the fire
Dancing your time in flight
Take us to a new height

<u>Just Wrong</u>

By
Raven Lotus Crow

When someone does harm
When someone isn't warm
When children are hurt
Being treated like dirt
When others want others canceled
And evil is all they channeled
When animals are kicked
Now you really got me ticked

Mad Hatter

By
Raven Lotus Crow

Riddles I give and nonsense happens again
All is up and down with more strain
Have you heard about the raven
What are you cravin'
Looking at the time
Taking our tea away is a crime
To hell with the Red Queen
She is battier then you've seen

<u>Inner Voice</u>

By
Raven Lotus Crow

Is it evil or is it gentile
Does it try to take over like a back-seat driver in a
rental
Can you fight it or do you let it win
Are you a plane going into a tailspin
When it says you are worthless
Fight back and remind yourself you are priceless
Your path is what you make it
Be quick and seize it

<u>Narnia</u>

By

Raven Lotus Crow

Through the wardrobe into a sight
How is there any light
Follow the kind fawn
All the way to dawn
Jadis is crazy
She has a battle against many
Aslan does live
The crown to the kids he does give

<u>The Horsemen</u>

By
Raven Lotus Crow

Charging ahead with destructive force
Four beings on a different colored horse
Pale as a corpse
Scary of course
Three and one begun
It is the apocalypse at a run
All is dead
So be it said

Alcohol

By
Raven Lotus Crow

Fatal to others and will cause distress
All it does is make you a mess
Some think it is divine
All the trouble with just a bit of wine
Can turn your world up-side down
Will eventually give you a frown
Having a beer with friends
Can spell many ends

<u>Nicotine</u>

By

Raven Lotus Crow

Makes people without it jerks
Some kids crave it and steal it from store clerks
Is it worth the fix
To get yourself in the mix
Too addictive for its own good
Wasting money on it than getting food
I don't do you demon seed
I would rather have the weed

<u>Seltzer</u>

By
Raven Lotus Crow

Bitter after taste
Without a flavor what a waste
Carbonated water from hell
You eventually put me under your spell
How many times can I force
To try to like something bitter without remorse
When you have flavor you are the best
Something like Ice please be the model for the rest

<u>Ireland</u>

By
Raven Lotus Crow

Lands of beautiful green
All your people are not mean
Love the liveliness of your bars
Driving on the left side with your cars
Land of pure magick
A shillelagh is a special walking stick
Best vacation spot ever
Love land of my ancestors forever

<u>My Dad</u>

By
Raven Lotus Crow

Man, you have gone down hill
I have gotten enough of my fill
Why do you hate me so
I have done nothing to you bro
All I did was be born
Yet you don’t approve of who i am, I mourn
When I came out as a gay
You said that I would pay
All I wanted was to be loved
Yet you choked my soul, a beautiful dove
Why would you hurt me more
Forever disappointed in you forevermore

<u>Cars</u>

By
Raven Lotus Crow

Freedom to be who I am
Going to new places I can
Beautiful piece of machinery
How you’ve gone down in history
One day you will be mine
One day I will be fine
You bring me to places
Have to go through the paces

<u>Dryad</u>

By

Raven Lotus Crow

Tree folk of the forest

Dance the dance of Morris

Appearing as a beautiful girl

One of which a guy would want to twirl

Beware not to stray

Or your life dear Dryad will be at lay

Hair of matching vibrant colors of the wood

Dancing to the beat of nature is very good

<u>Faith</u>

By
Raven Lotus Crow

All you believe in
All you show that can be sin
All of the love from above
Soaring higher than a dove
Be it spiritually in nature
Or religion from your mother
Believe what is right for you
For you know what to do

<u>Raven</u>

By
Raven Lotus Crow

Black winged messenger
Following as a passenger
Striking intelligence and grace
Flying so brisk as if it was a race
A group of you are called a unkindness
If anything you are generous
Feathers the color of dark bark
Strikes the night and the dark

Lotus

By
Raven Lotus Crow

Sacred holy flower
Grow ever faster
Beautiful shades of green and pink
For your roots do sink
Roots a good food
If you are in a good mood
Picture of you is good medicine strong
Roots so good you can't go wrong

<u>Crow</u>

By
Raven Lotus Crow

Scary in a Hitchcock film
A murder of crows are not dim
Very intelligent bird of black
Crowds around the haystack
For together they will hunt
Will get what they want
Morrigan's other form
For when you see her you have won

<u>Being A Better Me</u>

By
Raven Lotus Crow

As I look back
I'd give myself a smack
But accepting things are good
Is harder than it seems it would
But now I am more of a positive man
So upbeat and more is the plan
I have a lot to thank everyone for
Giving me a chance and opening the door

<u>New Jersey</u>

By

Raven Lotus Crow

Drivers go crazy behind the wheel
Have to have nerves of steel
Beautiful gorgeous gardens and hills
Farms around the state with mills
Sarcastic people all around
I know they just like to play around
We have worth and we can tell
Staten Island, what's that smell

<u>My Home Country</u>

By
Raven Lotus Crow

Oh, the great red white and blue
How I miss you
How come is everything sad
We have never been this bad
Oh, great country of mine
Being here is divine
I love you more than you know
Time to pick yourself up and say no

<u>Proud</u>

By
Raven Lotus Crow

To all the troops of my home
To all the stadiums with a dome
To all the students who succeed
To all the alcoholics that kick the need of mead
To all of the people who stay from drugs
To all those willing to clean rugs
To all those who do care
To all those who are just right there

<u>Shout It Out Loud</u>

By
Raven Lotus Crow

When you know the lyrics and sing
When you hear the dinner bell ring
When all is joyful and fun
When you don't want things done
When you get on a ride
When all get you excited and you can't hide
Shout it out loud now we say
All is good and will stay

<u>Love Is Special</u>

By
Raven Lotus Crow

As I look into someone's eyes
I see that person's many disguises
What they don't know it seems
Is that what they need to do is follow their dreams
There is kindness if you seek
You can be strong and not necessary meek
For all you need now is someone there
Someone who's willing to be near you here

www.ingramcontent.com/pod-product-compliance
Lightning Source LLC
Chambersburg PA
CBHW050811250726
48653CB00006B/2156